Walking
in a
Landscape
of Words

Written and illustrated by

Pamela Hoxsey

Walking in a Landscape of Words
by Pamela Hoxsey
Illustrations by Pamela Hoxsey

The quotation on page 5 is from
Think on These Things by J. Krishnamurti
© 1964 Krishnamurti Foundation of America.

Published by
Edwin House Publishing Inc.
P.O. Box 128, Ojai, California 93024
805-646-6647

Printed in the U.S.A. by
Quebecor Printing

BOOK DESIGN BY DEBORAH KERNER

Library of Congress
Catalogue Number
96-61927

ISBN: 0-9649247-2-2

This book
is dedicated to

REED

"Rain on dry land is an extraordinary thing, is it not? It washes the leaves clean, the earth is refreshed. And I think we all ought to wash our minds completely clean, as the trees are washed by the rain, because they are so heavily laden with the dust of many centuries, the dust of what we call knowledge, experience. If you and I would cleanse the mind every day, free it of yesterday's reminiscences, each one of us would then have a fresh mind, a mind capable of dealing with the many problems of existence."

J. KRISHNAMURTI

Author's Preface

When a deep question is sustained, and the room is quiet, and outside the window nature unfolds its drama in wind and cloud, in branches, leaves, birds, butterflies, and the buzzing of bees, the mind may have an opportunity to observe its own play. Out of its observation words may cast their shadow on the page without intention.

And when the movement of nature appears to dance before the eye, and the ordinary view has been relinquished, perhaps a drawing takes shape, simply as an extension of seeing.

Walking
in a
Landscape
of Words

I

No poetry or prose
Can elevate the word.
It remains
the poor shadow
   of a ghost
Of observation.

Out of the silence
   we emerge
Gathering names
   about us
Noise and cloud, clutter
   and wind...
What happened to
   the silence?

3

Word and sound
Aren't born in the body
They ride on
    the vibration
Of infinity.

4

There is a going out
and a coming in. Words
fly on the wind of
sound.

But sound without
the word, vibrates the
heart and mind and
needs no definition.

Words of sound, on
the other hand, cough and
sputter, and sometimes soar,
but rarely do they vibrate.

5

What was the first word
   and why
Weren't the sounds of
   the universe enough
Weren't our ears full
   to throbbing and
   our tongues numbly
   amazed...
Was it pain?...
Or had we just
   grown weary
Of infinity?

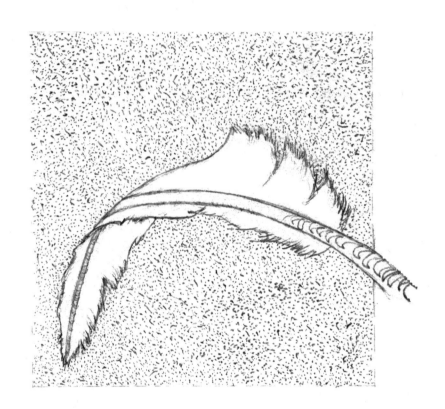

6

Songs seep out
    from the heart
And float through
    the night air
To greet the
    breast of the moon.

Is it possible to
view the world without
the veil of words?

To let the thunder
strike the bone and
shake with passion; or
to float on top of a
placid pond with no
cloud in the sky and
no need to fill it?

Is it possible to
observe with the mind;
to look out from an unknown
place and not abuse the
sight or sound or
silence?

To let the universe
play the body and mind

like the strings of an
instrument that is so
vast, empty, hollow, its
timber rings and throbs
with the stars.

8

When I wonder what
   will be
And look into the
   foggy realm of matter,
Do I create the reality
That steps fully formed
From out of the mist?

9

The body may sleep,
    but observation continues;
The body may die,
    Yet it is undisturbed.

Universes, stars, humans
    come and go
Yet, it abides.

Thoughts cloud;
Words obstruct;
We rarely glimpse
the presence that
is "not" us. It is
there but is not
loud like words, not
boisterous like thought,
not needy like desire.
It does not knock
on the door of our mind
And ask to enter....

Desires and gorging
    on
Every whim and experience
Send thoughts and
    heartbeat and
    breath
Racing.
But ever unsatisfied,
We spin on.
Reckless.
Torn with hurt and
    disappointment
And blind misunderstanding.

Softly waving in the wind
The young bird's
   feathers sigh.
Rigid sticks and
   cold minds
Brace against the harsh
   weather
But the bird sits
   warmly facing its
   brutality.

What is it that lives?

And what dies?

Only the drama being

    played out in the cells...

For that which truly

    lives,

Lets matter have its

    own way,

And dances and sings

    amid the spaces.

14

Sound

Silence

No whisper can spell
  its name
No name can contain it
Why try to squeeze
  it into a definition
Can't we live with
  the mystery?

Sweet nectar flows
    from that other's face
I drink in deeply
    and am lost in wonder,
Without knowing,
Who is breathing out
And who is breathing in.

Neither out far
Nor in near
It rests in that space
Where eyes, ears
   and brain
Come back to themselves
And the boundaries
of the cells
are eliminated.

We live our lives in
    fear of being hurt,
And hope to endure the pain
inflicted by others.

But we lack the
    imagination to see
that our own actions & theirs
are really one and the same.

The tragedies of our lives
    both real and imagined
grow from the deepest root
of false interpretation.

If I set out on a journey
    to discover something deep
and look out very far...
I will be disappointed.
If I look in very near...
Disappointed still.

Who is it that travels
    far and near?
Who is it that arrives?
The strings that follow
    out from me
Lead back only to myself.

The deepest deep,
Without destination,
Keeps no residence
and welcomes no traveler.

Anger arises when
   we're stuck
With feet in stone
   And tongues half-twisted.
Thoughts tear pathways
With their thorns,
then fall like ashes into dust.
Actions imprisoned,
burn like coal
behind the molten door
of the barren heart.

Weathered fingers flit
   like butterflies across
   the reeds of a basket
Patterns take shape
and colors blend
Serenading the eye
and the soul of the
   weaver
Who sits contented...

Where have the rest of us
gone wrong?

The world in its grandeur
Exploding with color
    and light and life
Beyond imagining.
Why do we close
    our eyes to it
And seek the
    entertainments of men?

Ever lonely
We seek understanding
Ever alone
We want others
   to fill the void.
Unable to face the vast
   emptiness
We cling to broken
   shards of relationship.

The stony face
and lack of expression
Wounds the heart
and echoes forlorn.

What lives there
Behind the walled in eyes?
Is it pain or is it cunning?
Has the fear of life
So blunted the blade of
pure emotion the
senses have turned to dust?

We take so much
credit for being
born as we are...
But what are we?

A human being is
    born into the world
and says
I am myself
Distinct. Unique. And separate.
But an acorn grows
into a tree, then other
acorns develop
seeking no individuality.

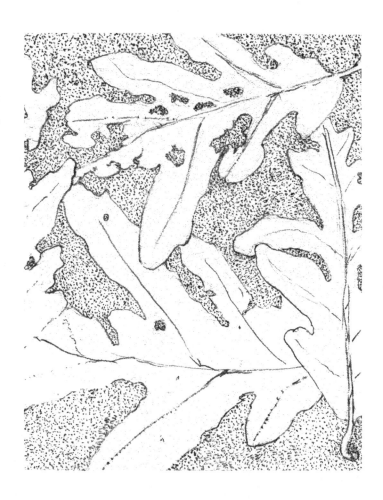

Some people ask
What is "enlightenment"
as though it is a
state frozen in time
Like a cloud ever still
   in the sky
Or leaves on a tree
   incapable of moving.

So long ago
A hurt was inflicted...
Is the memory correct
Or have new wounds
   and scars
Been woven into its tapestry

In this world, so full
   of promise, we
cling to hollow
Praises of love,
Ornate and
richly adorned like a
king's jewels,
But from a heart as
empty as a
beggar's cup.

30

Arrows of insult,
   death and disease
Why do we run from them?
Embracing the thorns,
Plunging deep into
   the ocean of pain
Brings calm
   like sitting in the eye
   of the storm
with no need to run,
no need to escape.
What wonderment!

The rain is falling...
but that's a myth...
For in a moment,
When the eyes blink,
It turns to snow.

A forest of memory
    lives in the brain
a thicket so dense
    little light can
    shine through
Is the sky one
    with the air
And can it touch
    the space between
    the branches?

Where is the life that
 we are living?
Is it in the body or
in the brain
Or is it between the
 molecules?
Without an edge
 Without meaning
Without a place
 Without end.

34

Savoring the song

which haunts the wood,

The shadows belie the cold,

and dusky smells

of damp earth

Greet the air

that flows in a misty

   stream

toward the winter horizon.

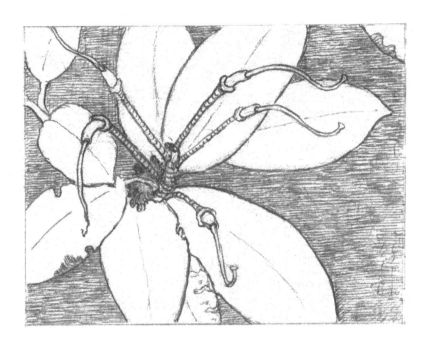

That old familiar thought
(I won't call it a friend)
Comes back to meet me
Again and again.
It repeats its program
and whispers to me,
Hauntingly,
Keeping its ties deeply
    imbedded
And forcing me to act
Without the least gurgle
of spontaneity.

There is
Presence
without movement
untouched by actions
    running in a maze
    like wildfires setting
    themselves in motion
But here
no tie exists
To going forward or
    moving back
and chaos only lives
    as an aside.

Living in a world
each of our own making.
Suffering the hurts
When our worlds collide;
We build the foundation
    of our beliefs
Stone by precious stone
    of hardened faith,
without a flash of insight
    to glimpse the castles
Built on air.

Were I to meet all
   and sundry
With a mind exposed
And chest unfettered,
Would they tremble
   with disgust
And hold their stomachs
   with two hands from
Foreign expressions and
   brutish honesty
That leaves them writhing?

For words of truth
Are bitter to the tongue
Even with self-paring
And who can live
   with feet standing
   on the hot coals of
Burning awareness?

What an impression
　　we make
on the surrounding air
and how pretentious.
Seldom do we listen
or sense the vast space
with us disappearing...

Thoughts batter the
   brain
like stormy waves
   bashing a sandy
   beach.
Tired, beaten, it
   waits for that
   time
When clear skies and
   quiet winds blow
cool reason and
   silence into an
   endless space.

To reside
   on the
   seat of truth:
Now thing.   No thing.

The first word. A sound.
Mimicking another sound. Trying
to capture it. Encapsulate.
Recreate. But failing. And then.
More words flow out like
spokes from a wheel. To
broaden the sense. Make it
understood. Rarefy it. Then
a web is formed. Threads
of meaning; shades of
intent. And the spiral moves
outward and further and
further away.

Until...

It has lost all the heart
of the first sound.

So...

With the first drop
of a pebble on the pond,
immense waves of meaning

begin to form and take shape,

with less and less relationship to it.

Then subsequent waves

are created from thin air,

having no weight, no measure.

And having lost all connection

to the first sound,

we can no longer tell them apart.

Which is the wave?

And which is the wave created from air?

43

Where sound and meaning
stand in for a thing. And
things take the place of
the real.

Where trees are not trees,
but abstractions. Where
symbols tell the tale. And
tales are woven on the
wind of sound.

Trees are no longer trees,
but myths.

Star words stand in
for stars.

And in this world we
live and die, as if this
world had breath and
heartbeat and vibration.

When I am quiet for a
moment and I observe the
breath, and the brain is
taking a rest from thinking,
the body seems to need to
make some physical adjustments
as though it just unburdened
itself of a heavy coat that
was out of balance and had
pulled the body out of
shape this way and that.

And in that silence
something speaks, but not
in words or thoughts or
even ideas. Only the energy
of pure being which has
no rope tied up to yesterday,
or tentacles reaching out to
tomorrow. There is ease and
calm and blessed emptiness.

And one wonders why
this being is always overtaken
again by the noise and desire
and punishment of thought.
How has thought grown
to be such a bully; from
where does it gather its strength?
    One senses the quiet is
always there even when
thought refuses to be
silent; like the quiet
of a night without wind
under the stars and the moon
being shattered by the loud
honking of a horn. Has
the quiet disappeared or
only been covered by one's
brutish ways?

45

We think it lies
   in a fine career
   or praises
from important others
   But oh so subtly
Life tells its tale
   in the swiftest
Glance of strangers.

46

Every whim and every
    urge
clutches at the wind
    and the world
is full
    of I's wanting.

47

Like an eye that
    focuses near or far

The brain defines
    the pathways
    of its limitations
If only I could let
    go of the eye
If only the brain
    would let go of me

Freedom in the universe
    might reign.

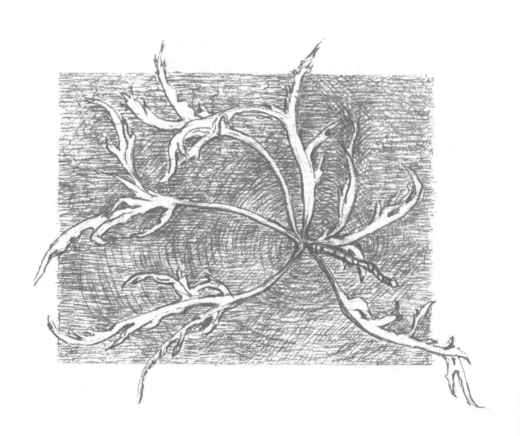

48

The feet are heavy
Trodding the earth,
And time fills the
   motion
With cement.

Where is our dignity...
   a quiet air...
Why do we have
   so much loud
   and garish need
for attention
Doesn't sadness break
   the heart
for losing, losing, losing
   our way?

Death...
What is it...
A word so fraught
    with fear
We tremble to look at it.

But what if
    it held no firmer grip
Than a smoky cloud
    rising up to
    greet the air
and after feathering out
    in the dancing wind
Leaves no trace
    upon the clear, open sky
    or the vast horizon.

The heart is touched
  with sadness
and what else
  can it be
to see what we've
  created
and keep creating
  endlessly....

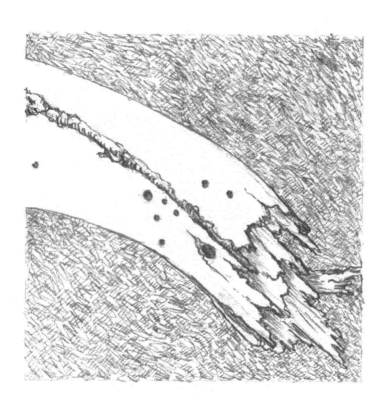

With faithful words
    we grip each
other's heart...
    but
Words are no more
    than sawdust
when our actions
    are not
    true.

This is the way I've been
    taught—to walk
in the world with
    certain shoes...
So now, when I look
    I cannot see,
when I listen
    I cannot hear.

Following a trend now
"living in the moment"
    but who
is it that lives
    and who
defines the moment?

Gold and silver
Fall like dust
Through clouds of mist
On a barren plain.

The forest and river
   are alive
   with
turtles like dark stones
   shining in the
   light
And birds fluttering
   and fanning
   their tails to
   find a pretty mate
And deer jumping
   through bright green
   foliage of May apples
   and columbine
Yet...there is silence....

The feathery blossoms
   brushed with white
Light the little tree
like a candelabra.

58

Bright sun sparkles
On the edge of the water
   of melting snow
Evaporating in magnificent
patterns on the concrete
   walk
But who can see
the fleeting beauty
When stiff presumptions
Crowd the mind with
knowing snow and water,
sun and walk?

The gift was given
   oh so long ago
And now you've died
   and it's come
   back
   to me...
Was it any gift at all....

White blossoms
    are raining down
    in the wind.
The watery crevice
    in the rock below,
    collects
and reflects them.

Droplets of water
   on a leaf
hearts circles pears
Divided by invisible
   boundaries
in the air.

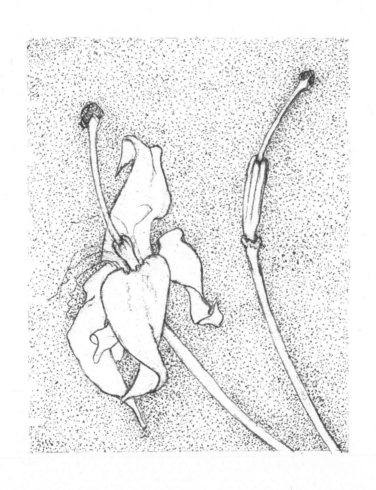

If seeing were filled
   with quiet
   breath and
endless pools where
   eyes once stood
What peace
   and purity arise
   there.

63

So far away from
    myself
I move endlessly
    searching...
If only I understood
    coming back

Watching the action
   of the self
   created
Putting the self in
   a circumstance
   to judge
Yet holding out
   another self
   untouched
Seems all so very
   absurd.

65

Thoughts are
like stormy
winds blowing
through the
mind.

Echoing across
   the void
In endless agitation
keeping the ball
   of thought
in motion
Spinning energy
   in futility.

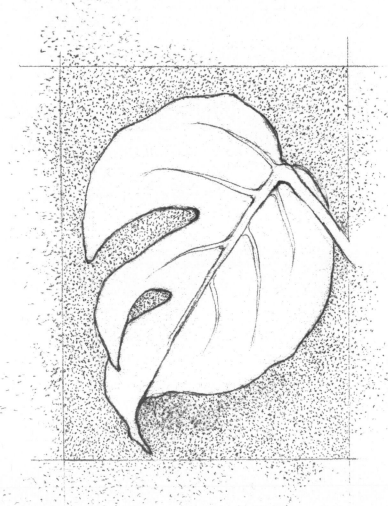

Hard winds blowing—
Pushing a thorny
   fist
   through the ear
With false words.

The energy is leaking
   rivulets are
   flowing out
always they
   are thoughts
Some attach and
   fixate outside
But once
   when tides were turned
and rivers changed their
   course
to meet in a place without
   a home
What fire burned there!

Definitions are like
   vises
They squeeze
   the life
   out of you.

Memories
Fashioned by matter
Regretting
Matter moved in other
    ways
Clinging
To form and creating
    thoughts of a life
That isn't.

Where in the world
   can we find clarity
With actions so pure
   the universe
     is
     mute....

I've often wondered
   at the senses
And now I am reminded
as the robin hops
   out in front
   of me
Gripping the shred of
   paper
   in his beak...
Are my eyes coming
   out to greet him
Or is he moving in
   to greet my eyes?

The feet stopped still
   to look at it
   It was so arresting
The palest pink buds
   glittering in the
   spring rain
Emerging
   With a shy blush
   from the
Delicate framework of
   its deep red arms...
Sometimes beauty is
   so overwhelming...
Are all the moments
   meant to be
   like this?

74

A sharp razor's edge
   of clarity
So clean is the
   blade of truth
it cuts through
   nostalgia, sweet ideas,
   false hopes and pain
And when the flesh
   is laid bare
to the universe
The heart sings, but
   without me.

I saw the mask
   lying on the
   sidewalk
floating in a
   shallow pool
I picked it up
   to take a
   closer look
and it melted away
   in my hands

Barely a breath escapes
    for
    watching it
Eludes perception...

The place where
   time does not
   exist

Allows all life and
   death to be
   together...

Brilliant ruby red jewel
   shining up from
the forest floor—
gently touched and
   turned to see the back
   of a black and
   dying beetle
so vulnerable with
   its belly held open
   to the sky—
choosing its own dignified
   way
   of dying...

We do not mourn
　　the wave
that rises and falls
and laps the shore,
　　and yet
we're no different
　　than the wave...
we just think we are.

The desire that
moves us to touch a
thing that's real; to
feel the rough bark
of a tree trunk; to
smell the scent of
a flower or hear a
bird's song—what
is it...

A memory
of illusion driving us
to recreate what was
once so beautiful,
we want to touch
it again?

Then, touching
it the thing becomes
known. Now it is

only bark, only tree,
only flower, only bird.
And we walk past
without a glance,
or opening the heart
to let it enter.

Then living
with the illusion only,
we weave a tapestry
of complex beauty
woven from the
nonexistent....

81

Sounds ring out
    from the body
    pulsating into the air
But instruments don't
    always need to
    sing
Sometimes they vibrate
    on the finest string
with some other's echoing.

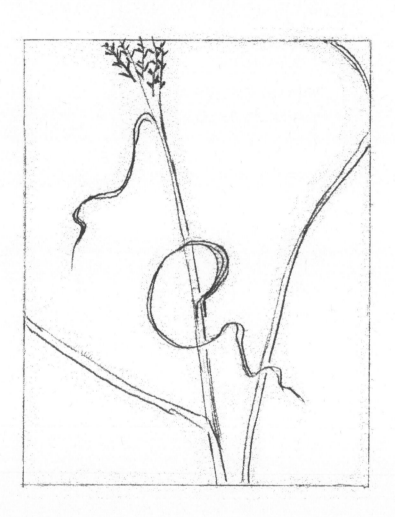

It may be hard
to listen to or accept,
but the whole of one's
life, with all of its
experiences, its highs and
lows, has no meaning
to the universe. This is
not depressing. It is not
negative thinking. It is
truly freedom....

When the breeze
   touches the hair
   ever so lightly
and the bird sings a
   gentle song
and a soft glow of
   fading light
   sweeps across
   the trees and hills
and quiet falls
   on all the earth
Why do men and women
   still stand shouting?

84

What if the life
　　were all
　　sound
Vibration through
　　the eye,
　　the mouth
　　the ear
And growing and
　　moving
Or even standing still
Pulsing beats on
　　a vast ocean
　　of silence.

85

There is a problem
   but I can't find it
my breath hovers
over the mountains
my eyes see
beyond the ocean
   and my hair
Mingles with the stars
And if I go
   in search
of the problem...
   it is so small...
I can't find it.

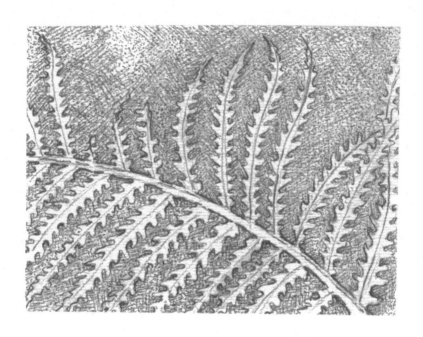

So quickly death
   steals the breath away
Leaving bone and
   muscle lying
heavily upon the ground,
closing the curtain
   on all our life's
   little dramas...
So suddenly uprooted
   are we
that the mouth falls
   gaping at its swiftness
   and
the brain stands silently
   wondering...
was it all a dream?

The Author

Ever since I was a child growing up in rural Illinois, I enjoyed contemplating the nature that was around me—like the water flowing over the rocks in a small stream that ran between our house and a wood, and the stars gleaming in the black country sky.

Later, I focused my attention on the arts: music, painting and drawing, literature, and the theater. For many years I searched for a way to fully express myself. And although I felt some growth occurring for me at this time, there was always a haunting sense that some depth of understanding was missing—an undercurrent which doubted the existence and authenticity of a "self". I became aware that my mind was fighting a constant duel as it tried to come to terms with its own contradictions.

From the first rough-edged look into the workings of my mind, I followed a path of questioning which lead me to ask: who am I; what is death; what is truth? The questions had a power and energy of their own. And as the questions moved in my mind, without my direction, they began to push against the hardened structures of my deepest beliefs. With the razor sharp edge of scrutiny came the destruction of many of my longheld beliefs, moving from the most obvious to the subtlest. Sometimes, a moment of what seemed to be a clearer perception came into view.

The questions have continued to move and change over the years, propelled by their own passion to reveal something new. This book was written from the observations that occur when such questioning takes place.

The text in this book was set in
Calligraph 421, a Bitstream font
designed by Georg Trump.

The text paper stock is
Teton Ivory, Felt Finish, 80 pound.

The cover paper stock is
Teton Tiara, 88 pound.